STEM IN CURRENT EVENTS

▸ Agriculture ▸ Energy ▸ Entertainment Industry ▸ Environment & Sustainability
▸ Forensics ▾ **Information Technology** ▸ Medicine and Health Care
▸ Space Science ▸ Transportation ▸ War and the Military

INFORMATION TECHNOLOGY

▶ Wearable Tech

▶ Talking Through Your Glasses?

▶ A Wireless World Promises Big Things

INFORMATION TECHNOLOGY

By John Csiszar

MASON CREST

Mason Crest
450 Parkway Drive, Suite D
Broomall, PA 19008
www.masoncrest.com

© 2017 by Mason Crest, an imprint of National Highlights, Inc.

Printed and bound in the United States of America.

First printing
9 8 7 6 5 4 3 2 1

Series ISBN: 978-1-4222-3587-4
ISBN: 978-1-4222-3593-5
ebook ISBN: 978-1-4222-8294-6

Produced by Shoreline Publishing Group
Designer: Tom Carling, Carling Design Inc.
Production: Sandy Gordon
www.shorelinepublishing.com

Front cover: Dreamstime.com: Aleksey Bolden top left; Weerapat Kiatdumrong top right; Everythingpossible bottom.

Library of Congress Cataloging-in-Publication Data

Names: Csiszar, John, author.
Title: Information technology / by John Csiszar.
Description: Broomall, PA : Mason Crest, [2017] | Series: STEM in
            current events | Includes bibliographical references and index.
Identifiers: LCCN 2016004804| ISBN 9781422235935 (hardback) | ISBN
  9781422235874 (series) | ISBN 9781422282946 (ebook)
Subjects: LCSH: Information technology--Juvenile literature. | Computer   science--Juvenile literature.
Classification: LCC T58.5 .C75 2017 | DDC 004--dc23
LC record available at http://lccn.loc.gov/2016004804

Contents

Key Icons to Look For

 Words to Understand: These words with their easy-to-understand definitions will increase the reader's understanding of the text, while building vocabulary skills.

 Sidebars: This boxed material within the main text allows readers to build knowledge, gain insights, explore possibilities, and broaden their perspectives by weaving together additional information to provide realistic and holistic perspectives.

 Educational Videos: Readers can view videos by scanning our QR codes, providing them with additional educational content to supplement the text. Examples include news coverage, moments in history, speeches, iconic sports moments, and much more!

 Text-Dependent Questions: These questions send the reader back to the text for more careful attention to the evidence presented here.

 Research Projects: Readers are pointed toward areas of further inquiry connected to each chapter. Suggestions are provided for projects that encourage deeper research and analysis.

 Series Glossary of Key Terms: This back-of-the-book glossary contains terminology used throughout this series. Words found here increase the reader's ability to read and comprehend higher-level books and articles in this field.

INTRODUCTION
What Is Information Technology?

Modern-day society depends on storing, retrieving, and sending information so much that an entire industry, known as information technology, has grown to service it. From the moment you wake up to the time you go to sleep, you probably access more information that you even realize. If you use a smartphone, surf the Internet, watch television, or listen to satellite radio, you're using information technology.

Humans have always needed to acquire and share information. While the information technology industry has come a long way since mankind ran around in animal skins and took shelter under twigs and branches, in the most basic sense, society's needs have not changed much. People still want to know the latest news, find their next meal, share information with others, and understand the world around them.

As in so many other STEM (science, technology, engineering, and math) fields, innovators in information technology have transformed the world. Easy access to information for all people has educational, societal, and global benefits, from the understanding of foreign cultures and traditions to the increase in global literacy. Similarly, the ability to transmit information rapidly has wide-ranging positive outcomes. It can help create a more productive workforce or just help people keep in touch. The consumer electronics industry has spread the information technology revolution to the masses. From social media apps such to smartphones with more power than the computers that ran the moon landings, information technology touches more humans around the globe than ever before.

The age of modern information technology began in the late 1870s, when American inventor Thomas Alva Edison developed the first electricity-generating station in New York City. Most people, and certainly scientists, were aware of the existence of electricity, in forms such as lightning and static electricity, long before the 1870s. However, the ability to generate and harness its power was a huge change. With a source of electricity, new information transmitters such as the telegraph and the radio were possible.

The 20th century saw an increasingly amazing series of inventions that used electricity. Many were connected to information, including the telephone, television, computers, and more. All of the STEM fields played an important role in the continuing evolution of information technology. More recent breakthroughs have included smartphones and cellular networks, personal computers, gaming consoles, global positioning systems, and satellite television. Most, if not all, of these industries have come to be considered indispensable to Americans in the 21st century.

Relentless innovation is one of the hallmarks of the information technology industry. Today's must-have, cutting-edge technology is often outdated in just a few years. For example, mobile phones that could simply place calls were an unbeliev-able invention when rolled out by Motorola in the 1980s. Today, even the most basic mobile phones can make calls, send and receive text messages, and connect to wi-fi networks at a fraction of the size and price of the original mobile phones. To keep up with the rapid pace of innovation, even industry-leading companies such as Apple must roll out updated versions of mobile phones every year or so.

As the information technology industry grows, new questions and concerns appear. Can networks and devices continue to generate faster delivery of information to satisfy demand? Can the ever-increasing reach of social media bring people together, or will it reduce the amount of social interaction? Can important data be protected from hackers and while stored or transmitted?

These and numerous other problems are currently being addressed by scientists, engineers, mathematicians, and other STEM workers to shepherd information technology into a new age.

What is Information Technology?

Whether the physics of electricity or the chemistry of batteries, basic science is at the heart of most of the advances in information technology.

SCIENCE AND
Information Technology

Words to Understand

client and server model   centralized computer network where clients request information from servers

DNA   deoxyribonucleic acid, the carrier of genetic information in nearly all living organisms

electromagnetic radiation   waves containing electric and magnetic fields that carry energy at the speed of light

genomics   study of the complete set of genes in organisms

geo-tag   an electric tag assigning a geographic location to a picture or video

mutations   genes with altered structures, resulting in variants that may be transmitted to future generations

peer-to-peer network   decentralized computer network in which all participant computers have equal status and responsibilities, as opposed to the client-server model

protocol   a set of rules governing the exchange of information between devices

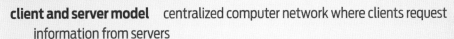

Although all STEM fields play an important role in the development of information technology, inventions would have little chance of success without basic science. The scientific process of asking questions, conducting experiments, and validating results is the foundation of all technological innovation. Science helps breed this innovation because it builds knowledge over time. One scientist might have a theory, but then other scientists will make discoveries based on that theory. For example, Scottish scientist James Maxwell first suggested the existence of radio waves back in the mid-1860s. Radio waves were not proven to exist until the work of German physicist Heinrich Hertz in the late 1880s. From there, it wasn't until Italian inventor Guglielmo Marconi created the "wireless telegraph" in 1895 that humanity had truly harnessed the power of radio waves. As is the case with most world-changing technology, the simple radio technology still plays a major role in today's society. While portable radios are no longer cutting-edge technology, a device you likely use every day—your smartphone—relies on the same scientific principles discovered by early radio pioneers. When you decide to make a call, your phone sends out a radio signal and looks for a nearby cell tower. Essentially, that tower then finds the phone you're trying to call, passes along the radio signal to the tower nearest the receiving phone and—*voilà*—your voice comes out the other earpiece, all courtesy of radio science.

No matter what the era, science is the driving engine behind the "gee-whiz" technology of the day. Shortly after Marconi wowed the world with his radio device, electricity was making its way through modern homes, and a vast array of consumer products was unleashed to the general public for the first time, from the telephone to the refrigerator. Transportation was on its way as well, with Henry Ford's Model A car and the Wright Brothers' first flight at Kitty Hawk both promising a new era of mobility. Today, global positioning systems, smartphones, the Internet, and other technologies are at the forefront of scientific innovation, but many still owe a debt to scientific laws and discoveries of

The Italian inventor Guglielmo Marconi created radio, a key forerunner to communication advances that have led to today's wireless world.

the past, proving that truly revolutionary scientific work has the capacity to transcend eras and international boundaries.

Radio and Global Positioning Technology

What is a radio wave, and why is it so important to modern technology? A radio wave is a form of **electromagnetic radiation** that conveys information in the form of sounds or pictures. An input device, such as a microphone, converts sounds into electrical signals that are carried in wave form. When these radio waves hit a receiver, such as an antenna, they are converted back into the sounds that were transmitted. When you use your mobile phone, you speak into a microphone that converts your voice into electrical signals; these signals, in the form of radio waves,

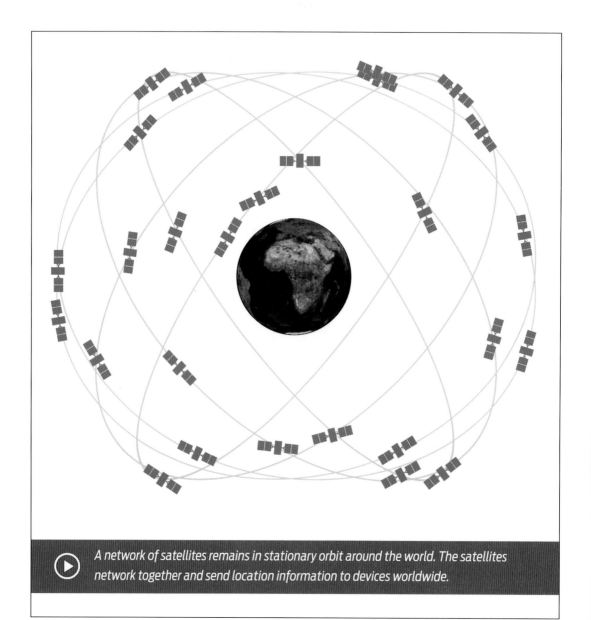

A network of satellites remains in stationary orbit around the world. The satellites network together and send location information to devices worldwide.

are then bounced among cell towers until they are received and converted back to the sound of your voice at the other end. That's why the sound of your voice can change when you call different people; some phones and cell networks are better than others at transforming the received radio waves back into the sound of your voice.

An inside look at how Global Positioning Systems work

Radio waves are also the core science behind Global Positioning System (GPS) technology. Most users probably don't think twice when they access an application like Google Maps. However, when you type in an address and search for directions, it's not your phone or your car that's providing the answer it's a network of some two dozen satellites orbiting the Earth that are doing the work. Each GPS satellite is essentially a big radio transmitter sending a signal that includes the satellite ID, orbital information, and a very precise atomic clock time stamp. A GPS receiver, such as the one in your smartphone or in your car's navigation system, processes the radio waves sent from the satellites and uses a mathematical formula to calculate the receiver's current location. Currently, the system uses between 27 and 32 satellites, with some being used as backups in case of failure.

Navigation is the most obvious product of the GPS satellite network. Today, nearly every form of transport, from ships to planes to the family car, uses GPS to navigate. Beyond navigation, the applications that have sprung forth from GPS technology are mind-boggling. GPS is vital for many military uses, such as the precise targeting systems used by missiles. Geologists use GPS

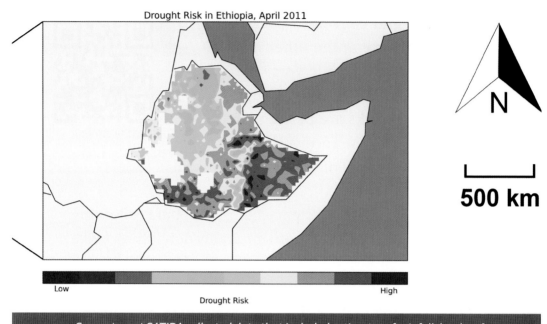

Drought Risk in Ethiopia, April 2011

Low · Drought Risk · High

Computers at SATIDA collected data that included estimates of rainfall, land surface temperature, soil moisture, and vegetation health to create this map of Ethiopia.

satellites for mapping and earthquake research. The financial services industry uses GPS time signals to help move money electronically. Hikers, cyclists, and other athletes use GPS signals to record workouts and distances traveled. Of course, GPS can also be used to **geo-tag** photos.

While there are lots of fun and productive ways to use your smartphone's GPS technology, scientists from the Vienna University of Technology are using it in trying to end famine. The process begins with GPS scans of the Earth's surface in areas likely to have drought and famine, such as the Central African Republic. Microwave beams, which are a form of radiation like radio waves, are emitted from the GPS satellites and are used to measure the water content of soil. Scientists then couple that data with information gathered from their smartphone app called "SATIDA COLLECT." This app allows users in drought-prone areas to provide research data to help determine famine conditions. Information collected includes how often people eat, what the current state of malnutrition is, and whether or not people have migrated from the area or died recently. Similar to the geo-tagging of photos, data uploaded to the scientists via SATIDA COLLECT is also assigned a GPS location. Combined with the satellite data, the scientists can then create a real-time map of areas where the risk of famine and malnutrition is highest. Such information is critical to aid workers, such as those at Doctors Without Borders.

Online Communication Advances

As big as the Internet is, there are still huge amounts of important data that are not available online. Scientists in

Internet by Balloon

Connecting the world's computers solves some problems but doesn't address how to get information to the millions of global citizens that still can't access the Internet. It may be hard to believe if you live in America, but roughly 60 percent of the world still lacks Internet access. Google's Project Loon envisions getting millions of these users on the Internet for the first time using helium balloons. The concept is that helium balloons can float to areas beyond the reach of cell towers. Within the balloons are solar-powered electronics that use radio waves to communicate with ground-based networks. The balloons travel through use of a balloon-within-a-balloon system; using computer data from the U.S. National Oceanic and Atmospheric Administration, Google can determine wind flow and direction at varying altitudes. By inflating or deflating the small balloon inside the larger one, the system is directed to the right spot. With such technology already in place, the 4.3 billion people in the world without Internet access may not be offline much longer.

Inventing the Internet

English computer scientist Thomas Berners-Lee was the first to crack the code of computer conversation. While working at CERN, the European Organization for Nuclear Research, Berners-Lee struggled to find a way to get information transferred from one computer to another. Ultimately, he realized that if computers could be programmed to follow two simple rules, they could exchange information with one another in a logical manner. In 1989, Berners-Lee dubbed his first rule HTTP, or HyperText Transfer **Protocol**. HTTP is a protocol using a **client and server model** for information exchange. You can think of an HTTP interaction between computers as a student asking a teacher a question and receiving an answer. The second building block devised by Berners-Lee, HTML (or HyperText Markup Language), is simply a process that lets the computer ask a question and to understand the answer it receives.

California are working to resolve that problem. David Haussler, a scientist at the University of California, Santa Cruz, is the founder of the nonprofit Global Alliance for **Genomics** and Health. Along with the Alliance, Haussler is working on developing a **peer-to-peer network** that would allow sharing of genomic data. More than 200,000 people have already had their genomes sequenced, providing a large sample size of biomedical data. This information can be used to compare the **DNA** of sick people from around the world. With that number likely to grow into the millions, doctors and researchers will have access to a vast pool of genetic information. For example, if you were unfortunate enough to develop cancer, your doctor would be able to run a DNA test on your tumor and compare it with others in the global genomic database. That could show the doctor what effect certain drugs had on others in your situation, along with the specific **mutations** involved in your tumor. Armed with this information, your doctor may be able to create a path of treatment for you. However, with this type of biomedical data not currently available on the Internet, a solution is needed. Haussler and other technical leaders at the Alliance have developed new procedures, file formats, and

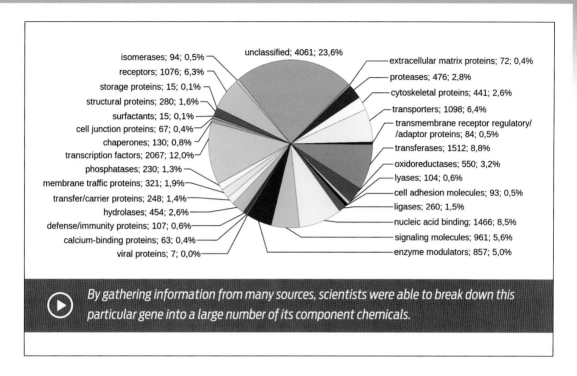

isomerases; 94; 0,5%
receptors; 1076; 6,3%
storage proteins; 15; 0,1%
structural proteins; 280; 1,6%
surfactants; 15; 0,1%
cell junction proteins; 67; 0,4%
chaperones; 130; 0,8%
transcription factors; 2067; 12,0%
phosphatases; 230; 1,3%
membrane traffic proteins; 321; 1,9%
transfer/carrier proteins; 248; 1,4%
hydrolases; 454; 2,6%
defense/immunity proteins; 107; 0,6%
calcium-binding proteins; 63; 0,4%
viral proteins; 7; 0,0%

unclassified; 4061; 23,6%

extracellular matrix proteins; 72; 0,4%
proteases; 476; 2,8%
cytoskeletal proteins; 441; 2,6%
transporters; 1098; 6,4%
transmembrane receptor regulatory/
/adaptor proteins; 84; 0,5%
transferases; 1512; 8,8%
oxidoreductases; 550; 3,2%
lyases; 104; 0,6%
cell adhesion molecules; 93; 0,5%
ligases; 260; 1,5%
nucleic acid binding; 1466; 8,5%
signaling molecules; 961; 5,6%
enzyme modulators; 857; 5,0%

By gathering information from many sources, scientists were able to break down this particular gene into a large number of its component chemicals.

programming tools to help move DNA data across the Internet. Their first effort was Beacon, a search engine that can access 20 publicly released databases of human genomes. With corporate Alliance members such as Google, Haussler is trying to expand this genome-focused network.

Psychology and Information Technology

Information technology isn't simply about the nuts and bolts of inventions. Since the goal of information technology is to transmit data among human beings, the science of psychology also plays an important role. While technological advances can make human life easier, better, or more interesting, how humans interact with this technology can change how it develops.

The Internet was originally used by scientists and the military to share and deliver critical information. Once the general public began to access the Internet, it became much more social in nature, and expanded dramatically. Whatever your interest is, you can now find a lifetime of information about it with a few simple clicks, from engineering to construction to how to use chopsticks. If you like to cook, you have access to a nearly unlimited supply of recipes; if you're an astronomy fan, you can tap right into the latest information from NASA. The Internet helps fulfill the psychological need that all humans have to satisfy their own curiosity.

The social aspect of technology has transformed how people interact. Psychologically, humans have a need to interact, a drive to feel that they belong. Social media sites such as Facebook and Twitter allow people from around the globe to share their thoughts on any subject they like, and others will "like" or "follow" those messages or even respond directly to the original author. That psychological need to reach out and be part of a community can now be achieved through virtual means.

While fulfilling psychological needs, there are dangers involved in spending too much time interacting with technology. The Internet, for all of its power, can also be a tremendous time waster. With so much fascinating information available at the touch of a button, it's very easy to get distracted from the real world and spend a vast amount of time jumping from link to curious link. For a species that is already prone to procrastination, having another way to avoid what needs to get done can be counterproductive.

A significant danger of social media in particular is that online interaction with others can replace real-life experiences with online "fantasy worlds." Some psychologists are concerned that humans are actually becoming less connected than ever, more attached to their devices than to human beings. Others feel the effects can be even more damaging, particularly in teens. A University of Glasgow study, for example, found that teens with high social media use, especially at night and involving emotional

Psychologists are conducting numerous studies about how we use technology and social media, looking for clues about how the devices are affecting our behavior.

social networking interactions, had lower self-esteem and higher anxiety. Another study in the journal *Cyberpsychology, Behavior, and Social Networking* found that those spending more than two hours a day on social networking sites were more likely to report mental health issues, up to and including suicidal thoughts.

Can the physical disconnection of social media cause psychological problems? As the wired world continues growing, we will have to face such issues with science.

Some branches of science are making enormous advances in information tech, but other sciences are helping us make sure we manage our use of it.

 Text-Dependent Questions

1. What form of electromagnetic radiation carries both mobile phone calls and global positioning satellite signals?

2. What is one of the benefits of studying genomics?

3. Name the Italian inventor of the radio.

 Research Project

Find statistics comparing the rate of Internet usage and also how many people have access to it in the United States compared to other countries around the world.

Never before have humans been as interconnected as they can be today. The ripple effects of networks of links, contacts, and associates is reshaping how we live and work.

TECHNOLOGY AND
Information Technology

Words to Understand

accelerometer   an instrument used for measuring acceleration

algorithms   sets of rules or instructions, typically used in computer programming

archivists   experts who work to restore and preserve old materials

end user   the individual actually using a product

gyroscope   a mechanical device using a rotating wheel to aid in navigation

HDMI   a standard for connecting high-definition video devices

heads-up display   a projection of information onto a windshield or visor

magnetometer   an instrument used for measuring magnetic force

Miracast standard   a wireless display standard for mirroring one screen to another

polarized   a method of restricting light waves to one direction

nformation technology spreads most rapidly when it translates scientific achievements into products that consumers, businesses, and governments can use. Current developments in information technology draw from both the basic scientific principles behind older inventions and from the ability of technology leaders to meet the needs of individuals and businesses. Once scientists have conceived and tested a scientific breakthrough, creators in technology fields take those proven principles and create products for the **end user** that can evolve with the times.

Smartphone: 3D Evolution

The smartphone has come a long way from 2007, when Steve Jobs of the Apple Corporation introduced the iPhone and promised, "This will change everything." According to *The Economist* magazine, more than 80 percent of the adult American population will own a smartphone by 2020. Part of the reason for this growth has been the evolution of the smartphone into a multifunction device. While the fundamental function of the smartphone still relies on radio technology, the iPhone kick-started the transformation by presenting an easy-to-use, attractive interface that combined three devices into one—an Internet connectivity device, a music player with touchscreen controls, and a user-friendly mobile phone. The adoption of the smartphone as the technological device of choice had reached the point that, as of 2015, more people searched for information using Google on a smartphone than on a computer, and more people shopped on Amazon using their devices as well.

Unbeknownst to many users, the average smartphone is already chock-full of devices and sensors that are paving the way for future innovations. For example, did you realize that your smartphone already likely has a **gyroscope**, an **accelerometer**, and a **magnetometer**? These features allow your phone to know its orientation and movement. How about pressure, temperature, and humidity detectors? Samsung worked those into its Galaxy S4 phone. Future phones are likely to build in electrical and health sensors to detect everything from air quality to your heartbeat. Many phones are already certified on the **Miracast standard**, which is essentially an **HDMI** over wi-fi connection, allowing you to project anything on one device—such as photos on your smartphone—to another compatible device, such as a television. In the future, smartphones are likely to become even more aware

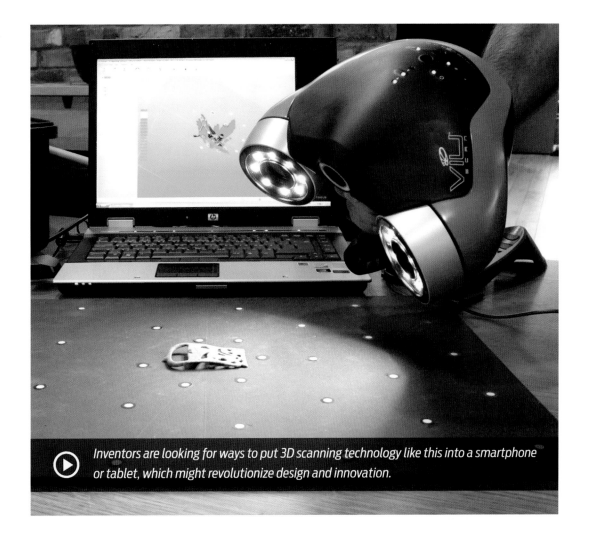

Inventors are looking for ways to put 3D scanning technology like this into a smartphone or tablet, which might revolutionize design and innovation.

of their surroundings, with the ability to interact with devices such as coffee machines or garage doors. Smartphones might even be able to message or call you with their location if you lose them or leave them behind.

While all these innovations are remarkable, the next revolution created by the smartphone might be in the field of 3D scanning. It essentially allows a user to take a 3D "picture" of an object. After capturing all the information about the shape and size of the object, the 3D scan can be used to create a real-world,

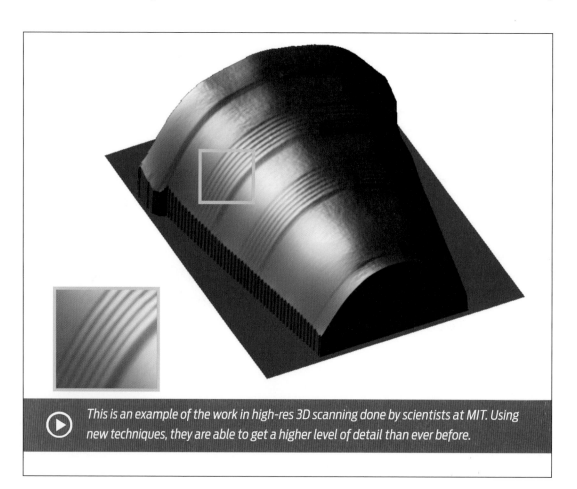

This is an example of the work in high-res 3D scanning done by scientists at MIT. Using new techniques, they are able to get a higher level of detail than ever before.

3D model of the original. High-grade 3D scanning has important ramifications for a number of industries. Museums, for example, could build replicas of their collections so that users could touch and feel artifacts without damaging the originals. Creating a portrait of a person would no longer require a sculptor to create a bust or a painting from an image. Cultural **archivists** could preserve assets and distribute them to the world's researchers and museums.

Make your smartphone into a 3D hologram projector

At the ETH Computer Vision and Geometry Group in Zurich, researchers developed the first app for a smartphone that allows users to create 3D scans of objects. MIT scientists followed this up with a technique that can increase the quality of conventional 3D scanners by as much as a thousandfold. Their work could allow for images from miniaturized 3D cameras housed directly within a smartphone. The MIT system, called Polarized 3D, combines a **polarized** lens with a Microsoft Kinect, a machine that can help gauge depth in an image. The resulting 3D images are even more precise than those obtained with a high-precision laser scanner. By incorporating this technology into a smartphone, everyday users will be able to create their own 3D scans.

Google Glass

The ever-increasing drive to make smartphone technology more portable, convenient, and powerful led to the development of Google Glass. Released to select individuals in 2013, Google Glass

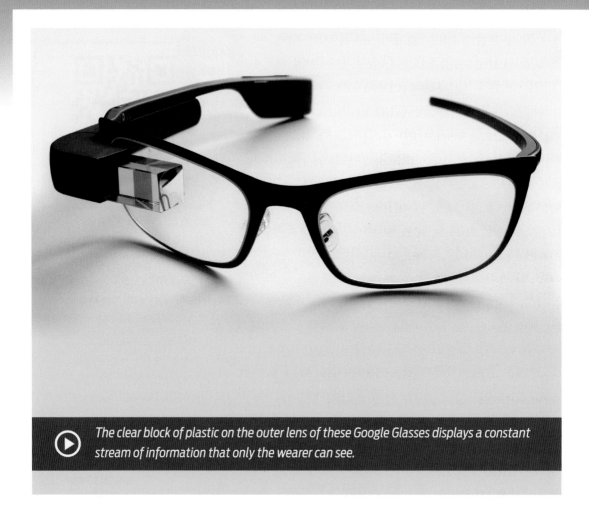

The clear block of plastic on the outer lens of these Google Glasses displays a constant stream of information that only the wearer can see.

is a **heads-up display** with the powers of a smartphone that can be worn like eyeglasses. Users can move objects in the heads-up display by utilizing a touchscreen mounted on the side of the glasses. For example, using the Google Glass touchscreen you could scroll through weather reports, phone calls, text messages or other important data, just like you would on a computer or smartphone. Google Glass is at the forefront of a new era of devices using wearable technology. By simply tilting your head or tapping the touchscreen, Google Glass allows voice commands to control the system. For example, you could command your Google Glass to "call John," "take a picture," or "record a video," as Google Glass also comes with camera and high-definition video capability. For information that is read back to the user, special technology and speaker placement allow the user to hear the information without it being audible to others nearby.

Much like the apps you can download for your smartphone, Google Glass offers numerous software applications, with most being created by third-party developers. Some of the more interesting Google Glass apps allow for facial recognition, photo manipulation and sharing to social networks, and various exercise and travel apps. Google Glass has also proved its value in the health care field. As more and more health care records are stored electronically,

Wearable Technology

The wearable technology industry is still in its infancy but seems destined to be a technological leader in the years to come. Wearable tech refers to any gadgets or clothing items that transmit or record information. Fitness tracking bands made by companies like FitBit are able to record physical activity and transmit that information to other devices, such as smartphones, typically via a Bluetooth connection. Smart watches, such as the Apple Watch, bring the technology of a smartphone into the casing of a watch, allowing you to check email, receive text messages, or access social media from your wrist. Fitness clothing and even implantable devices are likely to grow in importance as the wearable tech industry evolves.

Google Glass can access patient records and check live patient vital statistics. Google Glass has also been used by doctors to share video with other doctors during surgery.

The Google Glass program was temporarily halted in 2015 as revisions were made to the capabilities and price of the unit, which sold for $1,500 when first unveiled. The new device is expected to have numerous enhancements, including the ability

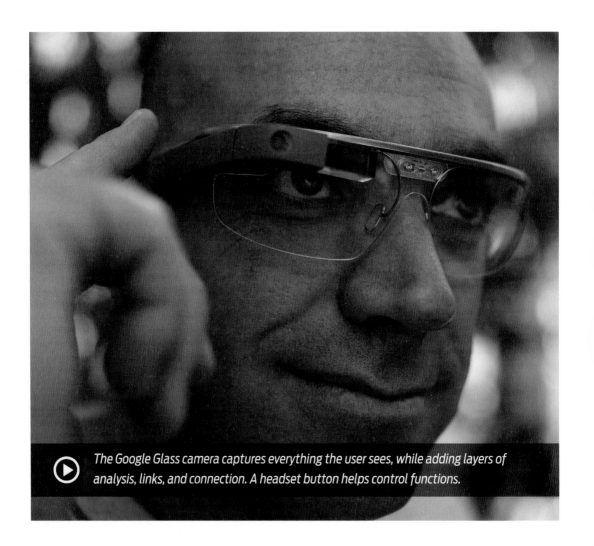

The Google Glass camera captures everything the user sees, while adding layers of analysis, links, and connection. A headset button helps control functions.

to fold like a typical pair of glasses, enhanced wi-fi capability, more durability to protect against falls, and a waterproof coating. Other improvements are likely to include a faster processor, a better camera, and a bigger display.

Bluetooth Technology

Bluetooth technology is a powerful, futuristic technology that has its roots in the simple radio science of Marconi's wireless telegraph. Invented by Dr. Jaap Haartsen in the mid-1990s, Bluetooth allows for the easy, wireless connection of various devices using radio waves, typically with a range of about 100 yards. Transmissions are low-cost and low-energy, and the wireless nature of radio waves often makes Bluetooth more practical than using wired devices. For example, one of the most common uses of Bluetooth is for streaming music. With Bluetooth, you can send music from a computer or other device to a wireless speaker across the room without the need for the yards of cables and wires required by old-fashioned stereo systems.

In fewer than 20 years, Bluetooth has transformed from a simple short-distance wireless connection into the industry-standard technology behind many consumer and commercial products. Nearly all modern car manufacturers now integrate Bluetooth technology throughout their vehicles, allowing users to make calls wirelessly, send text messages, or even access smartphone apps. The future of Bluetooth lies in complete integration with all aspects of human life.

A close-up look at Bluetooth technology

Baron Biosystems, Ltd., has developed an intelligent gear selection system that uses Bluetooth to determine the optimum gear for cyclists as they are riding. KitchBot created a Bluetooth-enabled thermometer that allows users to control slow cookers or other devices using a smartphone app. The Fliegl Tracker, a device invented by Fliegl Agratechnik GmbH, allows harvesting vehicles to communicate with one another using Bluetooth to track the complete farm-to-store cycle of grains and other foodstuffs. These and other products demonstrate how the basic science behind Bluetooth has evolved into technology that can help solve real-world problems, one at a time. But can Bluetooth grow to the point that it serves as a multi-faceted personal assistant?

Israeli technology company OrCam believes that vision of the future is already here. With the development of its product MyMe, OrCam has gone one step beyond Google Glass to create a fully integrated Bluetooth assistant. Users attach a tiny, unobtrusive camera to their shirt or belt to give the Myme its "eyes." Based on the inputs received by the camera, a computerized voice, powered by an artificial intelligence (AI), will speak via a Bluetooth earpiece to help a user analyze and interpret the world around them. The camera can also data to a smartphone or watch. For example, if you want a record of your eating or fitness habits, the MyMe can record your daily activities and send the compiled data to you for analysis. If you're at a meeting or conference, MyMe can send important information about people it "sees" in its cam; if you don't know a person who is walking up to you, a quick glance at your device can give you the information you need. The MyMe also has the power to analyze and interpret facial expressions of people you speak with and give you feedback about the encounter. OrCam considers the MyMe an "augmented attention" device that can help users acquire and respond to more information about their surroundings, and they are working with developers to leverage the AI features of MyMe even further. In an effort to combat privacy concerns, OrCam has programmed the MyMe to be an "on-the-fly" device that doesn't record any images or sounds.

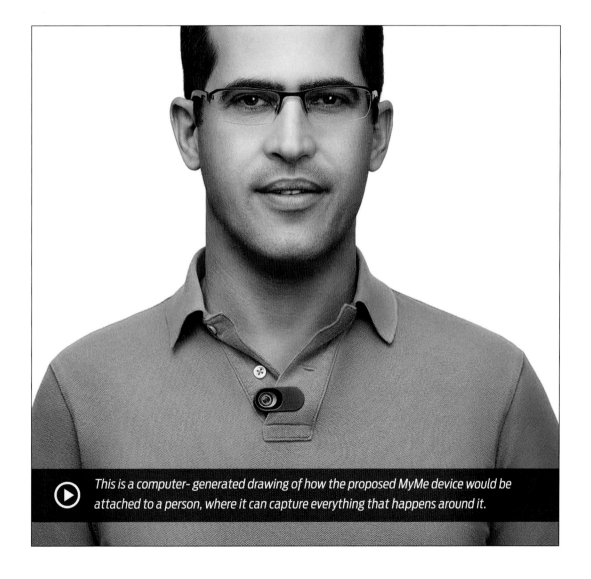

This is a computer-generated drawing of how the proposed MyMe device would be attached to a person, where it can capture everything that happens around it.

Driverless Cars

The concept of a driverless, or autonomous, car may seem like science fiction, but companies from Google to Mercedes-Benz to Audi have already put self-driving cars on the road. While the reality of driverless cars dominating the roadways is still far away, the technology to pilot a car without the need for human intervention is here. Some of the biggest obstacles to the development of the autonomous vehicle have been safety and legal concerns, rather than technological difficulties.

The technology behind the driverless car works in layers. The first layer is the global positioning system. Just like a human driver needs to know where to go and how to get there, so does the driverless car. But a simple GPS system isn't enough to actually drive a car. A second layer of radars, sensors, and lasers helps an autonomous car "know" exactly where it is on a road and what hazards or obstacles are around it. A camera works as the "eye" of the car, letting it "see" where it is going. Radar serves the same function during dark or adverse conditions, such as snow or rain. Lasers operate as a circular beacon, much like a lighthouse, giving the car constantly updated scans of its surroundings.

The third layer of technology in a driverless car is a complex set of **algorithms** that help interpret all the data that the car receives. Think about how complex the human brain is; for a car to be truly autonomous, it has to perform at that level of calculation, factoring in a multitude of variables in the blink of an eye. From the perspective of a car maker, this is perhaps the most difficult part of creating a self-driving car.

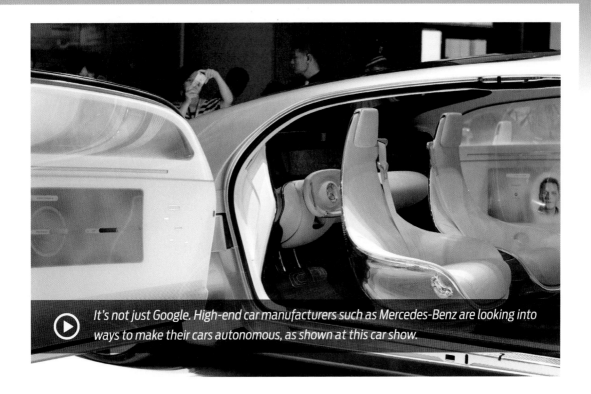

It's not just Google. High-end car manufacturers such as Mercedes-Benz are looking into ways to make their cars autonomous, as shown at this car show.

The last layer of the autonomous car is the ability to take all of the information it gathers and translate that into meaningful action, such as applying the brakes or making a turn. The computerized systems that translate such inputs already exist in most modern cars. The difference is that in current cars the input is provided by a human, whereas in autonomous cars the input will be data-driven.

The final push that may be needed to get self-driving cars from prototype to mass-market is real-time car-to-car communication. While radars and sensors in current vehicles can help a self-driver avoid accidents, the technology involved is very short-range and somewhat limited. For example, a sensor may be able to detect if a car is crossing into another lane or is about to hit a vehicle

One idea that might be part of a driverless future is to have each vehicle broadcast a constant network of signals so that cars can actually communicate with each other.

directly in front of it—but what if there's a danger coming from around a corner or behind an obstacle? Vehicle-to-vehicle communication, or V2V, seeks to answer those questions by providing self-drivers with a complete picture of their surroundings.

A pilot project conducted by the National Highway Traffic Safety Administration and the University of Michigan put V2V technology into nearly 3,000 cars and tested them in Ann Arbor, Michigan. The V2V technology allowed the cars to "talk" to one another by sending out information via radio wave. The cars shared data such as speed and GPS location up to 10 times per second to similarly equipped vehicles. After collecting and analyzing the data, the NHTSA estimated that more than 1,000 lives could be saved every year just in the United States. Plus, more than half a million accidents could be prevented. Of course, V2V technology is essentially worthless unless all cars have it; a single car equipped with V2V cannot communicate with non-V2V cars. As a result, the NHTSA announced that it wanted to make V2V technology mandatory in new vehicles as soon as possible. All major car manufacturers, along with car technology companies such as Delphi Automotive, are currently working on adding V2V technology to all their products.

 ## Text-Dependent Questions

1. What is the Miracast standard?

2. What are two products that make use of Bluetooth technology?

3. What is the main function of V2V technology?

 ## Research Project

Search the Internet and corporate websites to determine when Mercedes-Benz and Audi anticipate having fully automated cars available for sale.

Before the invisible work of wireless networks and cell phone transmissions can happen, the hard work in steel, wire, and cable has to be done on communications towers like this one.

ENGINEERING AND
Information Technology

Words to Understand

copper foam substrate   a porous form of copper, like a metal sponge

Instagram   an online photo sharing service

lithium-ion battery   a type of lightweight, high-energy rechargeable battery

micro-supercapacitors   battery-like electrochemical charging devices that can rapidly charge and discharge

terabytes   a measurement of computer storage size; 1 terabyte is equal to 1,024 gigabytes, or approximately 1 trillion bytes

USB port   a "Universal Serial Bus" device that allows data transfer between devices

voltaic pile   the first electric battery, developed by Alessandro Volta

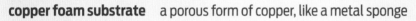

E ngineering in information technology refers to how specific technical problems are solved. While radio waves might be the technological precursor of mobile phones, for example, a handset without an engineered network is useless technology. Engineers create, develop, and build the background structure that enables the use of technological devices. Sometimes, the dividing line between technology and engineering is a fine one.

However, engineering generally refers to "big picture" technology, such as networks, towers, and systems, rather than smaller consumer devices, such as cell phones.

Mobile Phone Networks and Towers

While a mobile phone's ability to transmit voice and data via radio waves is a great idea, if those radio waves don't meet up with a receiver, they'll never make it to their intended destination. Cell towers are needed to capture the radio waves from individual mobile phones and transmit them to their recipients.

Connecting cell towers and networks is an immense engineering problem for a number of reasons. Radio waves can technically pass through walls and other barriers, but the quality of the transmission deteriorates. The purpose of a tower is to rise above an area so that there's a clear line of sight with as many cell phones as possible. That reduces the risk of dropped signals or bad connections. Since towers have limited range, enough towers have to be constructed so that as a mobile phone moves out of range it easily finds a new tower to continue its connection. This process is known as a "hand-over" and is processed by the switching center attached to the base of every cell tower. Well-engineered towers make these switches seamless to the point that you're unlikely to know when your call has changed towers. The entire system of cell towers and switching centers is an engineering marvel—but those times may be a-changing.

Steve Papa, founder of Parallel Wireless, envisions a near-term future in which massive cell towers become relics of the past.

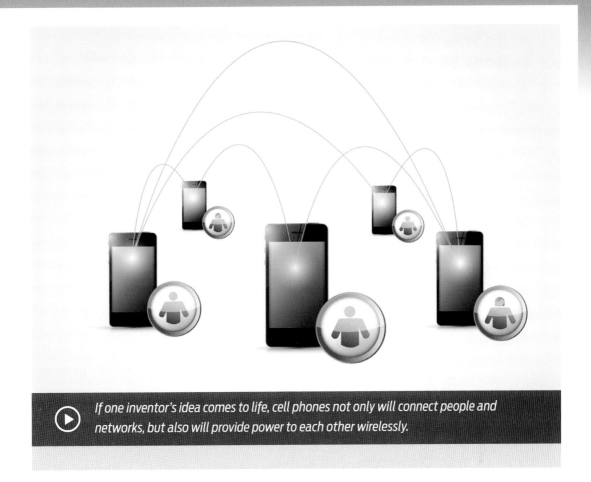

If one inventor's idea comes to life, cell phones not only will connect people and networks, but also will provide power to each other wirelessly.

In Papa's view of the world, individual mobile phones might become the next generation of cell towers. With mobile phones already being nearly omnipresent, additional towers would not have to be built if mobile phones could be engineered to receive and transmit nearby calls. Wireless telecommunications giant Qualcomm is already experimenting with technology that by-passes cell towers and allows cell phones within about 1,600 feet (500 m) to communicate with one another. With foreign partners Deutsche Telekom and Huawei, Qualcomm conducted a test of this system, known as LTE Direct, and hopes to roll it out soon.

So What Exactly Does 3G, 4G, and LTE Mean?

If you've ever seen an ad for a cellular network, you've no doubt heard the terms 3G, 4G, and LTE thrown around. Providers often make claims that they "have the nation's fastest 4G network." So what does it all mean?

When mobile phones were first developed, the original networks were only capable of sending voice calls, not data. This first generation of cellular networks was dubbed 1G. The first data transmission networks were 2G networks. While 2G networks were capable of transmitting data, speeds were often so slow that using a 2G network soon became impractical. The third generation of networks, 3G, was fast enough that users could send and receive data with reasonable speeds. The competitive nature of the mobile phone business soon led to 4G networks, also known as HSPA (High Speed Packet Access) networks, and 4G LTE (Long Term Evolution) networks. Carriers are in a furious battle to have the largest and best LTE networks, which can transmit data at up to 10 times the speed of 3G networks. And yes, 5G is on the horizon.

Batteries

Engineers are currently taking a relatively simple technology—the battery—and transforming it into a modern marvel. Batteries are essentially small-scale power plants that generate electricity using chemicals. While the chemicals and structure in modern batteries vary, most rely on the principles discovered by Italian scientist Alessandro Volta in 1800. Volta's first battery was known as the "**voltaic pile**," and it consisted of a stack of alternating copper and zinc discs separated by cardboard spacers soaked in salt water. Volta found that if he connected the bottom of the pile to the top with a wire, he generated an electric current.

Today, engineering in battery technology is focused mainly on smartphones and electric cars. While the **lithium-ion battery** has been the standard smartphone power source for years, engineers and scientists are working on other technologies to extend the life of battery-powered devices. Scientists at MIT have been working with Samsung to develop solid-state batteries that replace the liquid electrolyte in traditional lithium-ion batteries with a solid. According to MIT, these solid-state batteries aren't flammable and can be recharged hundreds of thousands of cycles before deteriorating. Solid-state batteries also have a high energy-to-weight ratio, offering 20 to 30 percent or more of the power of a similar-sized traditional battery.

As more and more people have become reliant on their smartphones to perform basic daily tasks, the need for rapidly charging batteries has become significant. Qualcomm has developed the "Quick Charge 3.0" that is the current standard in fast-charging

Inside just about every electronic device you own are tiny batteries like this one. Many of the biggest advances in technology are coming in power delivery and storage.

battery technology. Quick Charge 3.0 allows batteries to charge up to four times as fast as regular batteries. The engineering behind the process is dubbed Intelligent Negotiation for Optimum Voltage (INOV) by Qualcomm. This technology allows your device to more efficiently process the transfer of power from a wall outlet to the battery. Using Quick Charge 3.0, you can charge an average phone from zero to 80 percent in about 35 minutes.

Future innovations in smartphone battery charging are right around the corner. Rice University scientists have created

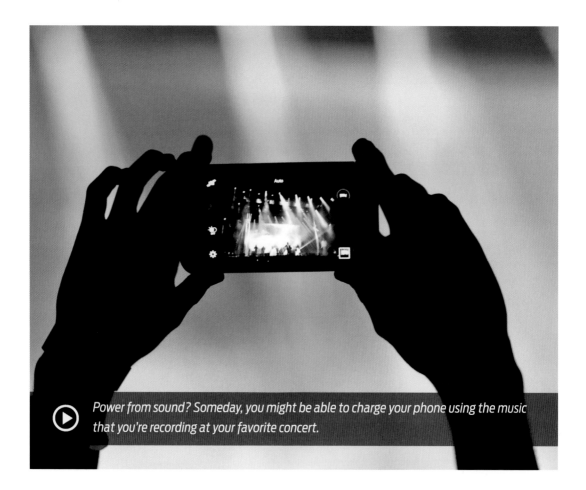

▶ *Power from sound? Someday, you might be able to charge your phone using the music that you're recording at your favorite concert.*

micro-supercapacitors by using lasers to burn electrodes into sheets of plastic. While too expensive to bring to market at this point, the resulting product could charge 50 times as fast as current batteries. Battery engineering is also moving towards nontraditional power sources. Scientists at Stanford University have developed an aluminum graphite battery that can reach full charge in just one minute. The company Prieto has developed a battery made out of a **copper foam substrate**. The batteries are safer, since there are no flammable components, they are fast-charging, and they carry five times the power density of the typical lithium-ion battery. They are also cheap to manufacture. Meredith Perry invented the uBeam, which can charge your cell phone over the air. The uBeam transmits ultrasound waves emitted from a five-millimeter plate through the air to your smartphone, which captures the beam and transfers it to usable electricity to charge its battery.

Engineers are working on even more fantastic ways to charge batteries rapidly and cheaply. Current experimental designs have been powered by radio waves, dew, sand, salt, hydrogen, solar energy, and even urine. But that's not all. The future of smartphone battery technology may be having no battery at all. Researchers at Queen Mary University of London have found a way to harness the power of sound to charge a smartphone. The scientists built a device covered with "nanogenerators" that collect sound vibrations and turn them into electrical currents. In experiments, the developers learned that traffic noise, music, and even human voices could trigger the electrical current in the phone, providing up to five volts of power.

In the world of electric cars, Israeli company Phinergy, in association with aluminum maker Alcoa Canada, has created an aluminum-air battery that has powered an electric car for 1,100 miles, well above the current average. Fuji Pigment is also advancing aluminum-air batteries for cars, creating the Alfa battery with 40 times the capacity of a lithium-ion battery and boasting a unique charging device: water. When its batteries are topped off with any type of water, the battery can remain charged for up to 14 days. StoreDot, a company birthed at Tel Aviv University, is working on a charging process using amino acids to create biological semiconductors. When completed, the company thinks it might be able to charge an electric car battery in just three minutes.

Data Storage Systems and the Cloud

While many parts of smartphones and personal computers are engineering marvels, data storage systems are the key to connecting modern-day devices. Before hard drives allowed you to store documents on your computer, for example, you'd have to print out anything you wanted to save. Advances in data storage technology have allowed for larger and larger storage systems at cheaper and cheaper prices, and they are far more portable to boot. It might be hard to imagine, but the world's first gigabyte-sized hard drive, produced by IBM in 1980, was housed in a cabinet the size of a refrigerator, weighed nearly 550 pounds, and cost about $115,000 in today's dollars! Today, of course, you can go to any consumer electronics store, plop down $90 or so and walk away with 2 or more **terabytes** of storage, all in the palm of your hand. Want even more portability? Thumb drives, so called because they are about the size of your thumb, can

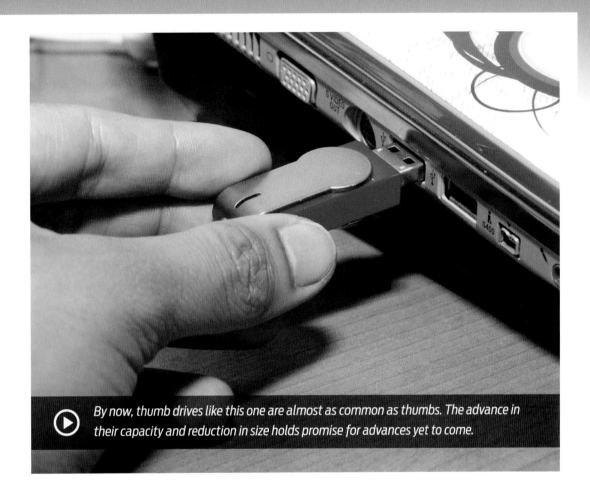

By now, thumb drives like this one are almost as common as thumbs. The advance in their capacity and reduction in size holds promise for advances yet to come.

be inserted into any **USB port** and can store 256 GB of data or more for less than $100. These extremely portable drives make the transfer of data between devices simple. You can copy your entire photo or music collection to a thumb drive, also known as a flash or jump drive, plug it into a computer or other device, and immediately have access to your copied files.

While engineering developments continue to allow smaller storage devices with larger memories, the true technological breakthroughs are occurring in the field of cloud technology.

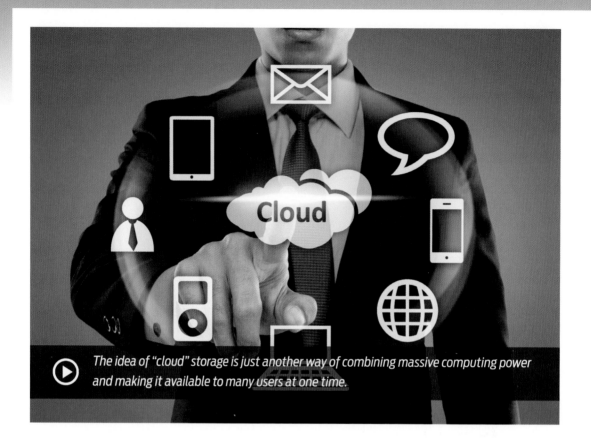

The idea of "cloud" storage is just another way of combining massive computing power and making it available to many users at one time.

"The cloud" is not one individual entity, but the catchy name reflects its function quite well. The cloud is a worldwide collection of servers. The engineering leap behind the cloud is that storage is moving from "hard" storage, like the hard drive in your computer or the thumb drive you carry in your pocket, to cloud storage on external servers. As with much of the technology you use, you may not even know when you are using the cloud. Any time you save data without using the physical storage of your computer or smartphone, you're likely using the cloud. For example, when you take a photo and upload it to **Instagram**, that picture is stored in the cloud. While Apple's "iCloud" storage service might give you a clue that it's a cloud-based service, if you backup your files using other services, such as Google Drive or Evernote, you're working with the cloud as well. The cloud is important to both consumers and businesses. Consumers benefit from extra storage of important data accessible from any destination; if you upload a photo or document to the cloud from your computer, for instance, you can retrieve that file from any other computer or smartphone just by logging in to your cloud account. Businesses benefit from cost savings, as they can rely on cloud servers to store their data rather than having to invest in costly on-site servers.

While connecting the world seems to be done by invisible beams, at the heart of the system are hard-wired, heavily engineered machines and systems that work behind the scenes to let the info flow.

 Text-Dependent Questions

1. Which is the faster network: 3G or LTE?

2. How fast can Quick Charge 3.0 replenish an average smartphone battery to 80 percent?

3. What is the "cloud"?

 Research Project

Visit the websites of AT&T, T-Mobile, Sprint, and Verizon to pull up maps of their LTE coverage in the United States. Determine which network has the most extensive coverage.

$$A_v = \frac{R_1 + R_f}{R_1}$$

$$\frac{10k\Omega + 100k\Omega}{10k\Omega} =$$

MATH AND
Information Technology

W hile other disciplines are vital to the growth of information technology, math comprises the very fabric of technological development. Without the ability to calculate, scientists couldn't understand radio waves, technology manufacturers couldn't build advanced features into smartphones, and engineers couldn't develop mobile phone systems. Mathematicians create the raw data that proves that certain technologies will work; they also design the complex solutions that help keep our data safe. Advanced mathematical applications have even grown to the point where they may be able to predict the future.

The ability of smartphones and networks to gather and display the data from stock market transactions has changed the way our economy functions.

Algorithms

Algorithms have been used for decades to help humans process and interpret data. "Algorithm" is a fancy word, but it simply refers to the steps taken or rules followed to solve a problem, typically by a computer. Even basic algorithms, such as the steps of a recipe, typically have a mathematical component, such as "add 2/3 cup water and 1/3 cup oil." More complex computer algorithms are built on advanced mathematics. For example, Google uses one of the world's most powerful algorithms to run PageRank, which determines how to rank web links when you conduct a search. Amazon uses algorithms to suggest items you might be interested in purchasing, based on the products you have looked at or bought on the site. The National Security Agency of the U.S. government uses high-level algorithms to sift through the countless bits of data it tracks from communications across the globe in its search for global threats.

Algorithms have taken on a new importance in the world of stock market trading. By programming information such as the price of a stock, its rise or fall in price, the number of shares traded, and other factors, a trader can develop an algorithm to automatically buy or sell stocks without the need for a human. Some market players, known as high-frequency traders, use algorithms to conduct millions of transactions per day, sometimes buying and selling a stock in a few milliseconds. In fact, high-frequency trading often accounts for more than half of the entire daily volume of shares traded on the major U.S. stock exchanges. High-frequency trading got a lot of press for triggering the "flash crash" of May 6, 2010. In just moments, major stock market averages plummeted briefly to ridiculous prices before rapidly recovering. However, algorithms are also used for trading by many major investment banks, **pension funds**, and mutual funds. Algorithms can work not only as a short-term trading vehicle but also as a risk-management tool by removing the element of human emotion from trading.

Encryption

Encryption has been important to humanity ever since the development of the written word. The ancient Greeks and Romans used simple **ciphers** to transmit coded messages. "Caesar's Cipher," used by Julius Caesar, simply shifted letters to the right or left by a predetermined number, so that "A" became "D" and "F" became "I," for example. In World War II, the Germans used the Enigma machine to keep data secret from the Allies, and it took a group of mathematical code-breakers to figure out the Enigma's algorithm. Today, encryption is part of the daily fabric of information technology, particularly when it comes to Internet security.

Advanced Encryption Standard, also known as AES, is a small variation on Rijndael, a highly advanced encryption algorithm created by Belgian cryptographers Vincent Rijmen and Joan Daeman. As of October 2000, it became the standard encryption method used by the U.S. government to protect vital national secrets. Essentially, AES uses high-level mathematics to break apart transmitted data into numerous pieces that are later reassembled by a code key. It's as if someone took "Caesar's Cipher" and applied a mathematical formula that made the transposition of letters and numbers infinitely more complicated. Without access to a key, data encrypted by AES is nearly impossible to access. You can think about encryption methods like a safe; documents are placed inside and cannot be read unless the safe is opened, either by a key or a combination lock. However, keys and locks are not always secure—cryptographic methods must always evolve to remain effective. Hackers and cybercriminals are constantly looking for weaknesses in encryption systems.

One of the problems with encrypted data is that it cannot be processed or analyzed until it is decrypted—taken out of the "safe"—but providing someone with the key allows them access to all of the data in the document. This can create privacy and

Perhaps the key security issue of the 21st century is the protection of data from hackers and from cybercriminals. Math and coding are front-line weapons in that fight.

security issues. For example, a company's database administrator may need access to personnel files, but the personal information contained within, such as employee salaries or Social Security numbers, needs to be protected. How can someone analyze encrypted files without having access to the actual document?

What Is a Hacker?

A hacker is someone who accesses computer systems without authorization. Typically, this involves using programming designed to defeat computer defenses. While hackers are not always malicious—some are simply kids or programmers out for the equivalent of a joyride—hacking has become a dark and growing industry, with hundreds of billions of dollars of trade theft occurring every year. Attacks on individuals often target passwords, financial information, and other private data. Corporate websites are regularly hacked in **denial-of-service attacks** or in attempts to steal corporate secrets. Government servers are prized targets, especially of foreign hackers, as they contain sensitive national secrets. Advanced mathematical encryption models are used to help defend against hackers, but no system yet created is entirely bulletproof.

The answer might lie in a technology that allows users to interact with encrypted data without actually deciphering the encrypted file. For example, a third-party could perform computations on encrypted data, such as the sales numbers or projections of a company, without seeing the actual numbers involved. While that may sound impossible, the problem may have been solved by research student Craig Gentry. Gentry applied a mathematical model to help make this type of encryption a reality. In its simplest form, a coded document is translated into a form usable by a third party. Once the third party performs its analysis or calculations, that information is translated back into a form applicable to the original document. While the mathematics can be overwhelming, the result is that documents can remain encrypted and yet still be available for processing; documents can remain in the "safe" and yet still be "read" by others.

If this works, then medical files could be sent to other doctors and hospitals without patient privacy concerns. Financial documents could be analyzed without revealing any "insider" information. Everything from voting records to search engine inputs could eventually operate under an additional layer of privacy and anonymity. As more and more data moves from personal storage to cloud computing, this math-based encryption could play a big role in keeping all of that information secure.

Math Fights Crime and Helps Patients

Mathematical models can be used not just to compute, but to predict. A joint study conducted by UCLA scholars and law enforcement officials managed to significantly reduce crimes rates

Information to help fight crime starts its journey when police officers enter it into their in-car computer terminals.

in the Los Angeles area over a 21-month period. These results were achieved based on the creation of an algorithm using 10 years of police data and six years of mathematical research. In addition to using historical crime data to help determine the future location of serious crimes, the algorithm was programmed to "learn" as it processed new, real-time data.

Emergency dispatch workers depend on technology to do their jobs. The math behind their work drives larger decisions, such as where to locate police stations.

The algorithm proved itself by competing against human crime analysts. In the first phase of the test, human analysts were given a map of the entire police district every day for 117 days. They were asked to indicate where crimes were most likely to occur within a specified 12-hour period. The crime-fighting algorithm managed to predict the locations of crimes more than twice as often as the human analysts. In the real-world application of the study, police officers were dispatched on random days to patrol areas selected by either the human analysts or the algorithm. The test was blind, meaning neither the patrol officers nor their commanders knew whether their orders came from a human analyst or the computer algorithm. As in the first phase of the study, the mathematical algorithm resulted in the reduction of more than twice as many crimes as the human analysts. In addition to lowering crime, the study suggested that the use of the predictive mathematical algorithm could save Los Angeles $9 million per year in court, victim, and societal costs.

Researchers at the University of Illinois at Chicago have stretched the boundary of what a predictive mathematical algorithm can do by creating one that can interpret what you *intended* to do and taking its own corrective action. For example, stroke patients often have to struggle against their own bodies to complete certain tasks. The algorithm developed in Chicago seeks to overcome that problem by analyzing a person's actions and determining their intention. The study hopes that the algorithm can power what it dubs a "psychic robot," or a machine that helps complete a task calculated to be the original owner's intent. In the case of the stroke patient, this could translate into a prosthetic that helps reduce or eliminate shakes or tremors if a patient is intending to

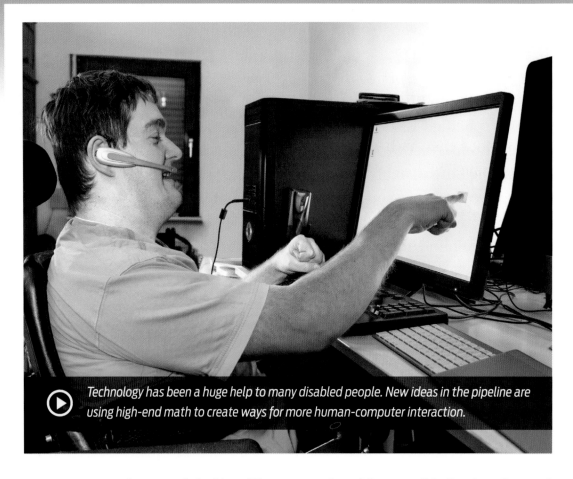

Technology has been a huge help to many disabled people. New ideas in the pipeline are using high-end math to create ways for more human-computer interaction.

move in a straight line. The same algorithm could also be plugged into a car's electronics to help steer the car in accordance with the driver's wishes. For example, if you're driving in a straight line down a road but suddenly slip on a patch of ice, the algorithm may be able to help the car correct its path and return it as soon as possible to its intended straight-line path.

Science and math lay the foundation; engineering and technology turn ideas into realities. Together, in the world of information technology, those realities are changing the world. Who knows what might happen next?

Text-Dependent Questions

1. What is an algorithm, and how might one be used?

2. How does the math-based encryption described help solve privacy issues?

3. In the UCLA study, was the predictive algorithm more or less effective than the human analysts at predicting crime locations?

 Research Project

Find a website explaining how to use "Caesar's Cipher" and translate a written sentence into a coded version.

Find Out More

Books

Rettberg, Jill W. *Seeing Ourselves Through Technology: How We Use Selfies, Blogs, and Wearable Devices to See and Shape Ourselves*. New York: Palgrave Macmillan, 2014.
A professor examines the impact of information technology on social interaction and personal well-being.

Wilcox, Christine. *Careers in Information Technology*. New York: Referencepoint, 2014.
A look at the training needed to work for companies making advances in information technology and online services.

Websites

The National Center for Women in Technology has resources for students and professionals looking to broaden their knowledge of the field.
www.ncwit.org/resources

This website offers online lessons and classes, many of them free, in a wide range of programming and technology subjects.
alison.com/learn/information-technology

This news-gathering site pulls together a huge variety of technology news, headlines, lists, links, and more.
www.cnet.com/

Series Glossary of Key Terms

capacity   the amount of a substance that an object can hold or transport

consumption   the act of using a product, such as electricity

electrodes   a material, often metal, that carries electrical current into or out of a nonmetallic substance

evaporate   to change from a liquid to a gas

fossil fuels   a fuel in the earth that formed long ago from dead plants and animals

inorganic   describing materials that do not contain the element carbon

intermittently   not happening in a regular or reliable way

ion   an atom or molecule containing an uneven number of electrons and protons, giving a substance either a positive or negative charge

microorganism   a tiny living creature visible only under a microscope

nuclear   referring to the nucleus, or center, of an atom, or the energy that can be produced by splitting or joining together atoms

organic   describing materials or life forms that contain the element carbon; all living things on Earth are organic

piston   part of an engine that moves up and down in a tube; its motion causes other parts to move

prototype   the first model of a device used for testing; it serves as a design for future models or a finished product

radiation   a form of energy found in nature that, in large quantities, can be harmful to living things

reactor   a device used to carry out a controlled process that creates nuclear energy

sustainable   able to be used without being completely used up, such as sunlight as an energy source

turbines   an engine with large blades that turn as liquids or gases pass over them

utility   a company chosen by a local government to provide an essential product, such as electricity

Index

Credits

(Dreamstime.com: DT.) Hugo Felix/DT 8; Brittanica/Wikimedia 11; NASA 12; Courtesy SATIDA 14; Human Genome Program 17; Antonio Guillem/DT 19; Monkey Business Images/DT 20; Mik3812345/DT 22; Creative Tools, Halmstead 25; Courtesy MIT 26; Mikepanhu/Wikimedia 28; Aleksey Boldin/DT 29; Loic Le Mur/Wikimedia 30; Courtesy MyMe 32; Tempestz/DT 35; Wikimedia 36; Oliver Sved/DT 38; Alexmillos/DT 41; Radub85/DT 43; Darko Dozet/DT 44; Emuted/DT 47; Odua/DT 48; Lisa F. Young/DT 50; Denphumi/DT 52; BawegPhotos/DT 55; David R. Frazier Photolibrary/Alamy 57; David Skalec/Wikimedia 59; Belahoche/DT 60.

About the Author

John Csiszar is a freelance writer and article curator. After graduating from UCLA, Csiszar was a registered investment adviser for 19 years before becoming a writing and editing contractor. In addition to writing thousands of articles for online publications, including The Huffington Post, he has created, edited, and curated a variety of technology-oriented projects, from web pages and social media text to software help manuals. Csiszar lives in Hermosa Beach, California.